Tackling the SPAM Me...

Dueep Jyot Singh

Mendon Cottage Books

JD-Biz Publishing

Disclaimer

The information is this book is provided for informational purposes only. It is not intended to be used and medical advice or a substitute for proper medical treatment by a qualified health care provider. The information is believed to be accurate as presented based on research by the author.

The contents have not been evaluated by the U.S. Food and Drug Administration or any other Government or Health Organization and the contents in this book are not to be used to treat cure or prevent disease.

The author or publisher is not responsible for the use or safety of any diet, procedure or treatment mentioned in this book. The author or publisher is not responsible for errors or omissions that may exist.

Warning

The Book is for informational purposes only and before taking on any diet, treatment or medical procedure, it is recommended to consult with your primary health care provider. **Our books are available at**

1. Amazon.com

2. Barnes and Noble

3. Itunes

4. Kobo

5. Smashwords

6. Google Play Books

Table of Contents

Introduction

For all those, who cannot do without their computers, especially the Internet, spam happens to be a part and parcel of their daily life. The real meaning of spam is to describe tinned meat, which is made up of ham. Well, the modern-day version of spam – 99.9% ham and 1% hot air – is you getting unsolicited and irrelevant messages and others such associated junk on your computer, smartphone or tablet.

SPAM could stand for Shifty Persistent Asinine Mail

These messages are sent through software to a large number of users, and are mostly concerned with advertising, spreading malware, phishing, etc.

For example, you just open up your email mailbox. You are going to get a number of emails, which are unsolicited. In fact, there is this desperate female called ADRIANA , who saw your face on the Facebook, and wants to get in touch with you. She wants to get in touch with me too. She wanted to get in touch with my 15 year old nephew too. My 68 year old ex-boss also gets a message from her, every few days.

All of us are on different computers. But Adriana says that she found us all so fascinating, she really, really wanted to be friends with us – irrespective of the fact that neither my nephew, boss, or I have bothered about a Facebook account.

This is just one version of spam. Anybody who has a Hotmail address is going to be tormented by ADRIANA. Anybody who has a Google address is going to be bothered by some other cutie who saw your face on the Facebook and really, really, wants to be a friend.

Around 10 years ago, spam was just beginning to make its presence felt. Advertisers had just found out all about the power of the Internet as a medium for advertising their business and making people aware of their products. At that time, 62% of the total Internet email was spam. In 2003, it was 45%. In 2015, it is a whopping 87%. This junk email, or spam, is now one of the most taxing issues for the Internet service providers, as well as for users.

Not all of these unsolicited emails are business related. More of them are clever Internet scams, disguised as pertaining to come from your bank, telling you about some unusual activity which has been seen in your account. They want to confirm that you have not done any particular transaction, which has caused such a red flag in their system.

All they want of you, is to click on the link given below, and reach their website to reassure them that everything is on the up and up.

So what do you do, you are so worried? You click the URL link, and you are taken to a web page, which looks like your banking site's web page.

You are now requested to login.

The moment you do that, you have had it. Somebody crouched in a cellar somewhere in the remotest corner of the earth has all your personal details at his fingertips. Beats hacking into your banking account, doesn't it?

Consider this to be the modern version of the Plagues which assailed Egypt in the days of yore. Like a swarm of locusts, you find yourself inundated with email, and spam mail, which you never solicited. But you are going to be blessed with it, merely because you have an email address.

So How Does a Spammer Benefit by Sending You Spam

Now just imagine you have been sent a message from let us say JPMorgan, asking you to make sure that you have not done any transactions which have caused their systems to go haywire. I do not have an account with the this bank so I know it is a scam. However, you have an account with this bank.

Naturally, you are worried. So you click the button given in the message.

What happens then?
The spammer has immediately got access to your email address, which means that you are now going to be inundated with more mail. That is because you have already validated your email address.

You have also given them access to your personal information and password, and my, my, all that lovely money in your own bank account. Say good bye to your hard earned money, it is going to be shifted through E-banking or a bank transfer, into an unknown account, because your particulars are in the hands of clever hacksters.

Access to even one bank account out of the millions of mails sent free through the Internet is going to make all that effort well worth it, don't you think? And you would be surprised to know there are a number of people, who instinctively click on the URL given in the mail, instead of going straight to their bank's secure website and clicking on it to check the status of their account.

Viruses and Malware

Apart from cluttering up your email inbox or junk mailbox, spam is also a potential and powerful source of viruses and malware. So, you may ask, why would anybody want to send a virus to you. Is there something wrong with their mental makeup? Believe it or not, most of the viruses sent to you are going to be from companies who are selling antivirus software.

It is a well-known fact, leaked out accidentally, on purpose, by one of the major software companies. They had one research team making viruses, and another research team making the antidote for the same virus. Both would be perfected. And then the virus would be sent all over the world. An artificial panic would be created, with a lot of hullabaloo being made of the threat to computer security. And then [fanfare and trumpets] the company would come out with an antivirus software, costing just $99!

Thanks to the publicity, everybody would rush to buy that antivirus, for a virus made in their own labs, by their own people!

This totally unethical and ruthless marketing stunt is about the same thing as a number of multibillion-dollar funded pharmaceutical companies doing research on mutated bacteria and viruses, and their effect on human beings in other parts of the world. And then, they can market the antidote drug – to combat that particular ailment, in that particular region at a highly inflated price.

If the virus got back to their own countries, hey, buy the drug and who bothers about the mortality rate.

Consider the Ebola/swine flu/avian flu and AIDS viruses, to be exactly like computer malware and other electronic viruses developed in research labs and kept under supposed control through expensive drugs/antivirus programs.

Apart from being offensive, spam is always fraudulent. The email address of the recipient is going to be procured from the Internet without their consent. It is also going to put a strain on the time, resources, and productivity of corporate networks and ISPs.

Recognizing Fraudulent Spam Messages

Apart from lottery scams, there are other fraudulent messages which clutter up your mailbox every day.

So how to you recognize them?

Any message which does not have subject matter in the subject area is going to be spam. Unfortunately, these spammers have understood that point, and that is why they are going to write a couple of words in the subject area. Not only does this satisfy the subject area requirements of the mail provider, but it helps make that message look important to you!

Very important message in all capitals! Did you notice that Basil , who is so eager to give away so much money to me, through the kindness of his heart does not know my email address? He does not even know my name , but I am Dear:. Sometimes you might be a dear one in these messages!

This message was sent through a spamming software.

After that, you are going to be requested to supply your personal information to him. Believe it or not, there are fools born every day, who fall under the category of stubborn fools, and who will not listen to good advice, telling them not to give any sort of personal information, including your name, email address, bank details, phone number, and so on to anybody on the Internet.

That person may have excellent credentials. He may be as pure as the driven snow. But do you give the car keys of your Mercedes-Benz to any person who admires it and wants to take it for a test drive? Not unless you are mentally or alcoholically impaired.

Consider giving this personal information to people on the Internet to be on par with these actions done under the influence of both above said states of mind.

All legal documents to back up your claim as the deceased Next of Kin will be provided. All I require is your cooperation to enable us seeing this deal through and I guarantee that this will be executed under a legitimate arrangement that will protect you from any breach of the law if you are willing to help in this claim. Please get back to me with the below information to enable us proceed.

If you are interested Please get back to me,

YOUR FULL NAME_____
YOUR ADDRESS_____
YOUR OCCUPATION_____
YOUR AGE_____
YOUR DIRECT TEL NUMBER_____

Best Regards,

Hon. Barrister Basil Igwike.

Spam is going to be related to products, financial services, and scams. Lately they have become really desperate, trying to sell me Viagra and Cialis at really discounted rates or to get me to sign up for adult related and pornographic sites. But then they know that they have a market for these products, so they are doing their marketing through spam mail.

Apart from posing a real threat to the viability of email, spam mail is becoming detrimental to the interests of e-commerce entities.

So here are some more ways in which you can recognize this sort of mail abuse.

The Internet's email system is a global phenomena, which in some ways is rather scary, because billions of dollars of e-commerce is invested in this particular method of communication. Anybody who has control over an email service provider has control over the world. He can gain access to the financial dealings/accounts/personal information/and other pertinent information which we humans so casually write down in our emails and which we send through electronic media, all over the world.

This means that we have given the rest of the world full permission to get access to all that information, regardless of their promising us that the email information is safe and secure. All that is bovine fertilizer; it has been proven that anybody can get access to anybody else's email, as the media reported, a while ago, as in the case of documents related to information and contracts. Senior officials in Microsoft had something to do with this scandal.

Spam can be considered to be the younger brother of agencies like email service providers and possibly Intelligence agencies. This information access, which they are still trying to justify, is just a patrolling of your emails without your knowledge. Spam is getting direct access to your information because you allowed it to do so by clicking the mouse.

In spam, the personal identity and context of the message sent to the recipient is a real event, because the message is equally applicable to many other potential recipients.

The recipient, who has definitely not granted explicit and deliberate permission to the sender to send that email. He/She then revokes that permission by clicking on the "unsubscribe" or the "remove" links found in the mail to get off a mailing list, this is not a good idea. Like I said before, you are going to be validating your email address and giving these spammers a valid identifiable email address.

If you need to unsubscribe from a mailing list, you need to go to the company or the enterprise's site and unsubscribe from there.

Any reception and transmission of the message which appears to give you a disproportionate benefit to the sender, because he is so altruistic that he intends to give away lots of money to you, and just 20% is going to be kept by him, well, this is a totally recognizable scam.

Just imagine walking up to a stranger with an apple in your hand. Tell him that you are feeling so altruistic that you want to feed him three fourths of the apple, while keeping one fourth for himself. You just want his name and address as proof that he fed you that Apple. His immediate reaction is going to be a holler for help for the police and for the loony bin. He is also going to wonder what is the catch , and is this some research test/program being done by researchers or Candid Camera?

Surprising that a person who is going to do that amount of thinking on the street goes completely blank when he is confronted with that same sort of trick being perpetrated through his junk mail.

And he goes around dreaming of all those millions and even pays large amounts of money as money transference and banking charges. Some months ago, a lawyer in our city got caught in one of these scams and paid out huge amounts of money to a company in Spain, which told him that he had won a state lottery ticket.

You have not bought a lottery ticket. And yet you expect to have won a huge prize in the state lottery sweepstakes, far, far away from your own country?

Who Are These Spammers?

I am not spamming dad, I was just contacting my friends on social media!

These spammers are out there, invisible, gloating over their computers in small towns and large cities, avidly collecting addresses from mailing lists, web browsers, webpages, chat rooms, forums, and any other available source. They have absolutely no social skills, because their lives are revolving over one overpowering and all-consuming obsession – firing away of enthusiastic messages in the hope that someone, anyone will respond.

Psychologically, they are misfits and do not have well-developed and mature emotional growth, especially in the matter of personal relationships and social interaction. They want to belong somewhere, and to show the world that they are very important. But they do not dare do that openly so they make best friends with their computers.

These messages are going to vary from "work from home – earn $10,000 in 30 days "or "Lose Weight Overnight!" or promising to give you access to the hottest Free adult sites on the Internet.

If you respond, you are going to see that there is absolutely no one to sell you the products or the services which have been promoted so enthusiastically and hyperbolically. You have just confirmed your email address. It is possible, that you have been put on some other spammer's list as a person interested in adult sites/wants enhancements in personal body parts/wants to lose weight, and so on and so forth.

In some cases, you are going to be instructed to send a particular amount so that they can send their wonder drug/pill to you or whatever products they are promoting.

Moral of the story – most spammers do not even sell a product or service. The reason? Most have a malignant mental attitude. Some of them may try to commit outright fraud, as in the case of asking you for your financial details. The reasoning here is, if there is some person out there, ready and willing to take a chance to buy this product and is really gagging for it, why not sell him his dream. After all, our product is as ephemeral as his dream.

These people have managed to persuade themselves that they are doing a public service to people, just by giving them some hope, incidentally, earning a bit of money on the side.

Email Marketing – Spam Effect

Once upon a time, marketers were thrilled with the idea of a global market for their products. Emails offered people all over the world, broader reach to wider and cheaper markets for better quality stuff. Along with that, there was quicker delivery, and easier consumer feedback for a lower cost than any other marketing medium ever thought of in the history of mankind.

So, people began to use emails to sell their products or services to other consumers on their emailing lists. These well-designed and professional emails had consumer related and relevant information along with product information, and options like subscribe or unsubscribe. You could also offer feedback on products. You could also place an order by email, phone, or online.

But then, when there is something good in the market, there is going to be some malign force somewhere trying to take cheap advantage of such a facility. These people got access to the names of the subscribers after finding out the sign-up information from these sites.

So again, they are willing to blame you for visiting a website and signing up there. After all, you were opening yourself up to spam, just by going to one particular site weren't you?

I do not understand how that particular mental reasoning works, but all these spammers know that they are doing something not acceptable by known professional, social and ethical standards. But man has always been able to persuade himself that whatever action he is doing is for the greater good of mankind!

Let me give you an example. I wanted the original traditional recipe of how the French made mayonnaise and went to a French cuisine site, where they asked me to become a subscriber. So I logged in. The traditional "recettes" (recipes) were interesting, but the very next day I found my inbox full of junk email in French!

This clearly meant that somebody had access to that particular site's mailing list and had got my email address from them.

I immediately went to that site and removed all my particulars from their list, site, newsletters, and so on.

The junk mail stopped immediately.

Of course it is very difficult for us to go to all the sites on which we have enrolled ourselves and we log in regularly to unsubscribe from their mailing lists. But you may want to do that for sites which you have not visited for the past 6 months.

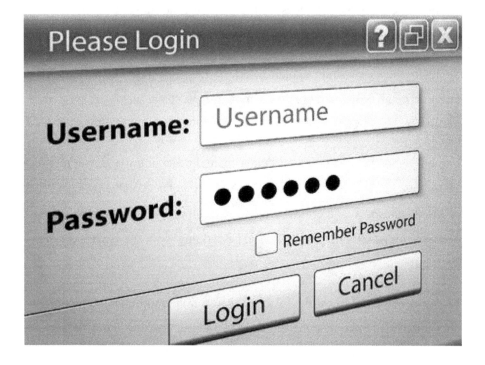

Also, there are plenty of sites out there, which say that they need money in order to keep your domain name. Only today I will send one of these messages telling me that I needed to pay $69 to keep my domain name for one of my websites. I would rather have that website domain name expire than pay these scammers/Pirates.

The ones who say they need money to maintain their website have given their website up to advertisers. These websites also have programmers designing their websites in such a way that the moment you click on the site – anywhere – a page is going to load on.

Any website which I have not clicked on, but which loads on by itself is definitely not a website to be trusted. **This includes a site called Jabong.** They are so desperate for people to buy from them that they are willing to appear on your screen in the website version of spam?

These sites include dating sites. They also include gaming sites and sites which promise you money, which you have been using in order to play card games on the Internet. After this, they are going to ask you for your credit card information in order to make sure that you are who you are.

Giving any sort of credit card information to any site out there is to be done at your own risk. You may find yourself canceling your card because of credit card fraud and identity theft.

Spam After Effects on Email Marketing

Due to the rising volume of email and spam, email marketing is possibly going to be a future nonviable marketing factor to generate more income and to get more potential clients.

Here is the reason why, 90% of my mail goes straight into my junk mailbox. I really do not have time to look at it, because I know that 99% of it is going to be junk mail. The important 1% of my emails are already going into my inbox. Emails sent by junk mailers are hardly opened.

Scare Tactics

There, I have just forwarded that email message on to 21 of my good friends, who need good luck...

Remember that even if the headlines are compelling, and making it sound like it is a life-and-death situation, if you do not open up the mail, the chances of the email being read are close to nil.

That is why spammers are getting to be really desperate, and are now sending out mail, which can be considered psychological warfare. This includes mail telling you that if you do not pass on the mail to 21 of your good friends, you are going to face bad luck immediately.

Believe it or not, there are plenty of people in the world who are so superstitious and who are so terrified of bad luck that they are immediately going to pass on that virus to their friends. One of the most powerful viruses of 2010 was attached to a simple email, which asked you to pass on the email to your friends, so that you could get continued good luck…

The sad thing about this particular virus is that you do not even need to open up the email. The moment your friend/colleague sends it to you, it is going to enter your system, and start multiplying unchecked like a cancer infection.

The only good luck you would get was, that in the next 30 days you had to buy a new computer, because the virus had junked the OS system/hardware. Naturally, this virus was thought up by a malicious soul with horrible viciousness in his mental and emotional makeup. But then, human psychology is the most frightening thing out there.

This is the reason why most website visitors do not sign up for mailing lists anymore. They are scared to give their email addresses out. They also fear that the addresses are going to be sold to 3rd parties, whatever the website owner may say, and their unsubscribe request is not going to be honored.

In fact, I know of a couple of sites, where you go in to unsubscribe and you are going to get a blank page with error 404. Needless to say, I never visited those sites again. Nor do I recommend them to my friends.

Many of us fail to distinguish between permission marketing and email spam. Spam is actually a major threat to legitimate email marketing. That is because a glut of messages is going to make the entire marketing medium less effective. In fact, it has already begun to have a detrimental effect on strategic marketing through email.

Protect Yourself from Spam

The moment I open my junk box in order to see if any of my important mail has been sent to it by mistake, I find plenty of spam. I click on all of those mails without giving them a 2nd glance.

Instead of sending it to my recycle bin, and cluttering up my space , I just go to the phishing scam button on my navigation bar. I do not know whether Microsoft has any ways of stopping this particular mail, coming from this mailing address but I satisfy myself that it is not going to be sent on from the server.

You may want to go to your email provider options and look at the junk options out there. Set them according to your own requirements. You may want the junk to go directly into your recycle bin. You can then check out your recycle bin once every 2 – 3 days, just on the off chance that some important message did not end up there.

Spam Combat Ideas

Tanks to the complexity of the direct email marketplace, the resourcefulness of the spammers is increasing every day. The global nature of the Internet also ensures that there is no single piece of local legislature or state-of-the-art technology, which will be able to stop spam.

Stemming the tide of the spam is going to require multiple and consistent complementary efforts from the IT technology community, marketing professionals, governments, email users, and the ISPs.

This of course is impossible because human beings are incapable of doing something in tandem without somebody else trying to shut them down.

In fact, in 2004, Microsoft and Yahoo Incorporated, which were the 2 largest email service providers in the world at that time began to think up an idea of charging email senders a small fee. Bill Gates considered this to be the best weapon to fight the rising tide of spam.

According to Mr. Gates, the problem would be solved in 2 years because of systems that would require people to pay money to send an email.

People immediately decided to cancel their Hotmail addresses and signed up for Google, which did not require a payment of money to send messages. Google immediately took full advantage of this marketing tentative idea and now is one of the top email service providers in the world, whereas, Hotmail has lost its credibility thanks to security leaks.

And the flood of spam still flows on unchecked, 11 years later.

So that means, you as a consumer, are technically the prime target and ultimate sufferer in the clash between legitimate email marketers and bulk email spammers.

Desktop Alert Applications and Programs?

I still have not found any good and reliable desktop alert software/applications/programs which allow mail to be sent directly to my desktop instead of being delivered to my inbox. Sending such messages have 2 benefits.

Firstly, the messages claim the desktop all to themselves. This virtually guarantees that they are going to be read and remembered. Secondly, users do not need to give their email or any other contact information in order to subscribe through email service providers.

In such a case, all one needs to do is simply download a small application. If you want to unsubscribe, you just uninstall the alert application.

Unfortunately, all of the desktop alerts which I have found online do not work well at all.

The CAN –SPAM Act

According to the CAN Spam act – the US government's anti-spam policy set up in 2003, [Controlling the Assault on Non-Solicited Pornography and Marketing Act], regulations were made which ordered email marketers to provide legitimate return addresses and opt out information in all emails they sent to email addresses.

However, this immediately set forth the whirlwind of opposition as users felt the law superseded stricter laws that allowed users to sue and prosecute spammers directly. According to spam exports, the new law underplayed the freedom of the users and provided technological loopholes for spammers to continue doing their business with impunity.

So CAN –Spam today is definitely disregarded and overlooked. There is absolutely no way in which spamming can be controlled effectively. Even though Microsoft designed address verification tools and Yahoo thought up domain keys to work within email management systems, along with filters to authenticate senders email addresses, spammers still flourish unchecked.

Eliminating Spam

And 99% of It Is Junk...

Eliminating spam completely from your inbox is impossible. So make sure that all your mail goes straight into your junk box. Except for the addresses in the inbox, giving you direct mail from your contacts, everything else should go into the junk mail to be removed automatically after a given number of days.

You will need to set that option yourself in your email service provider. Webmail service providers, like Hotmail, track junk mail. They have also created a special folder in which classified junk mail is taken without the intervention of the user.

This is the folder which I inspect every one or 2 days, and empty out apart from the mail, which goes directly to my "delete" folder.

You as a user can also block email addresses – either a particular sender or all mails originating from a particular domain. The only problem is that scammers use so many domains, especially with idiotic endings like mail@hotmale.com or mail@witehouse.gov, etc, that it is almost impossible to block all the domain names.

You may want to look at the latest email filtering and management services available on the Internet. Seriously speaking, like desktop alerts, I have not found a reliable email filter till date, so maybe someone may think up some really effective application/software, soon and make his billions.

The next tip is somewhat of a no-brainer. Stop publicizing your email address by signing up on every site you visit. So, all right, a site gives you the latest info on videos, games, celebrity gossip, fashion info, info about cars or what have you, but is it necessary for you to sign up? Cannot you see that site as a visitor?

If the site demands that you sign up, before you can gain access to any of their webpage content, navigate away from the site. There are plenty of fish out there in the Internet sea, giving you better information and content which you can browse as a visitor.

The more a particular email address is seen on Internet bulletin boards and in newsgroups, forums and in chat rooms, the more are the chances of you getting spam.

Conclusion

This book has given you lots of information on the menace of spam. Spam is unsolicited commercial and bulk email, which persists even after a consumer or user has opted out are unsubscribed from a mailing list. It has a deceptive subject line, message and header. It is going to come from a fraudulent or suspect source.

With the power of email comes the abuse of email in the shape of spam. Spam cannot be called marketing in its truest sense. This is not responsible email marketing

There is no stringent law anywhere, and the world, which regulates and controls the growth of spam. There is nothing which requires senders to disclose the origin of email messages. Laws have not taken a stand on prohibiting the sending of commercial email, even if it is sent without consent or without any sender information or with deceptive headings.

Therefore, to protect the privacy of individual citizens and the business interests of the e-commerce industry globally, regulation of spam needs to be tackled on a global war footing zone. Australia, UK and USA are trying their best to think up ways and means to prevent and legally regulate spam, but we still have a long way to go to prevent the spam menace from taking over our lives.

Live Long and Prosper!

Author Bio

Dueep Jyot Singh is a Management and IT Professional who managed to gather Postgraduate qualifications in Management and English and Degrees in Science, French and Education while pursuing different enjoyable career options like being an hospital administrator, IT,SEO and HRD Database Manager/ trainer, movie , radio and TV scriptwriter, theatre artiste and public speaker, lecturer in French, Marketing and Advertising, ex-Editor of Hearts On Fire (now known as Solstice) Books Missouri USA, advice columnist and cartoonist, publisher and Aviation School trainer, ex-moderator on Medico.in, banker, student councilor ,travelogue writer … among other things!

One fine morning, she decided that she had enough of killing herself by Degrees and went back to her first love -- writing. It's more enjoyable! She already has 48 published academic and 14 fiction- in- different- genre books under her belt.

When she is not designing websites or making Graphic design illustrations for clients , she is browsing through old bookshops hunting for treasures, of which she has an enviable collection – including R.L. Stevenson, O.Henry, Dornford Yates, Maurice Walsh, De Maupassant, Victor Hugo, Sapper, C.N. Williamson, "Bartimeus" and the crown of her collection- Dickens "The Old Curiosity Shop," and "Martin Chuzzlewit" and so on… Just call her "Renaissance Woman") - collecting herbal remedies, acting like Universal Helping Hand/Agony Aunt, or escaping to her dear mountains for a bit of exploring, collecting herbs and plants and trekking.

Check out some of the other JD-Biz Publishing books

Gardening Series on Amazon

Health Learning Series

Country Life Books

Health Learning Series

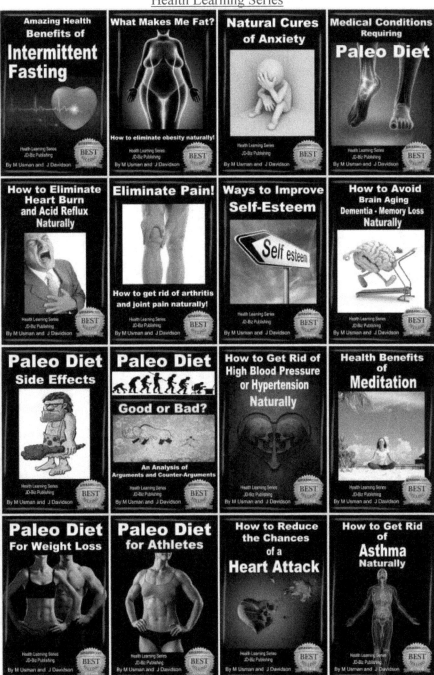

How to Build and Plan Books

Entrepreneur Book Series

Our books are available at

1. Amazon.com

2. Barnes and Noble

3. Itunes

4. Kobo

5. Smashwords

6. Google Play Books

Publisher

JD-Biz Corp

P O Box 374

Mendon, Utah 84325

http://www.jd-biz.com/

Mendon Cottage Books

P O Box 374, Mendon Utah 84325

http://MendonCottageBooks.com

Learn to Draw Series –Learn to draw beginner books teaching you how to draw with step by step instructions.

Health Learning Series – health education series covering nutrition and what foods can do for you to keep you healthy and active.

Amazing Animal Books Series– Children's fact books about all kinds of animals.

Survival and Prepping Series – Books covering everything from food preservation to survival skills.

Healthy Gardening Series – Books teaching you all the basics to growing and harvesting your own food.

Plan book Series – Books on how to build everything from chicken coops to houses.

ISBN 9781516988648

90000 >
9 781516 988648